piece by piece productions
Young Vic

Francesca Moody Productions and piece by piece productions
in association with the Young Vic present

OHIO
by The Bengsons

Developed in collaboration with Actors Theatre of Louisville
Initial development in collaboration with Sarah Gancher

Ohio was commissioned and developed by piece by piece productions and was first produced by Francesca Moody Productions and piece by piece productions at Assembly Roxy Upstairs as part of the Edinburgh Festival Fringe in 2025, followed by a UK tour performing at Bristol Old Vic and the Young Vic, directed by Caitlin Sullivan.

Supported at the Young Vic by the Season Circle and The Charlotte Aitken Trust

CAST AND CREATIVE TEAM

Created and Performed by The Bengsons

Director: Caitlin Sullivan
Scenic Designer: Cate McCrea
Projection Designer: David Bengali
Lighting Designer: Bethany Gupwell
Sound Designer: Nick Kourtides
Associate Director: Lydia Cook
Associate Scenic Designer: Ceci Calf
Associate Video Designer & Engineer: Dave Murray
Associate Lighting Designer & Programmer: Oscar Burr
Associate Sound Designer: Dan Samson
Access Dramaturg: Alison Kopit
Production Manager: Jack Boissieux for JBPM
Associate Production Manager: Emma Vize for JBPM
Production Assistant: Ida Pontoppidan for JBPM
Production Sound Engineers: Aidan Good & Liam McDermott
Production Electrician: Alexander Hannah

Produced by **Francesca Moody Productions** and **piece by piece productions**

The team for the Edinburgh Festival Fringe 2025 run includes:
Company Stage Manager: Leon Smith
Deputy Stage Manager: Chloe Forestier-Walker
Sound No 1: Hope Brennan
Sound No 2: Christina Spanoudis

The team for Bristol Old Vic and the Young Vic 2025 run includes:
Company Stage Manager: Chloe Forestier-Walker
Sound No 1: Hope Brennan

Special thanks to:
Andie Burns, Anna Spence, Anne Kauffman, Benjamin Atkinson for Helios Media, Christabel Holmes, DMLK, Emma Horne, Erica Rotstein, FlybyNite, Ian Kagey, Infinity, Jess Chase, Joy Burkland for Zanni Video, Michelle Mangan PR, Mihaela Bodlovic, Norwich Puppet Theatre, Stage Sound Services, Sydney Price, Whitelight

ABIGAIL BENGSON & SHAUN BENGSON | Performers

Abigail and Shaun Bengson are a married composing and performing duo raising two children in NYC and Vermont. They believe grief and joy are the same thing. They are interested in anything that gets us all free.

The Bengsons made their Broadway debut in *All In: A Comedy About Love* (Hudson Theatre).

They wrote and performed *Ohio,* for which they won The Scotsman Fringe First and was the Runner-Up for the Popcorn Award (Edinburgh Festival Fringe, Bristol Old Vic, Young Vic); *The Keep Going Song,* for which they won the Obie Award for Sustained Achievement (LCT3, Actors Theatre of Louisville); *Sovereignty Hymns* (La Jolla Playhouse); *Oh Courage* (The Joyce, international tour); *My Joy Is Heavy* (Arena Stage); *Hundred Days* (La Jolla Playhouse, New York Theatre Workshop, US Tour); *The Lucky Ones* (Ars Nova); *Where The Mountain Meets The Sea* (ATL's Humana Festival, Manhattan Theatre Club); *Anything That Gives Off Light* (Edinburgh Theatre Festival, US tour); *Hurricane Diane* (Two River, NYTW); *You'll Still Call Me By Name* (New York Live Arts, Jacob's Pillow); *Sundown Yellow Moon* (WP Theater); and *Iphigenia In Aulis* (Classic Stage Company).

They were recognized with a 2024 Obie Award for Sustained Achievement in Performance and have received the Jonathan Larson and Richard Rodgers Awards, as well as nominations for the Drama Desk, Drama League, and Lucille Lortel Awards.

The Bengsons are proud to be NYTW Usual Suspects.

CAITLIN SULLIVAN | Director

Caitlin Sullivan is a New York based director and theatre maker.

Upcoming credits include: *The Last Medicine Show* (Ars Nova); *Calf Scramble* (Primary Stages); and *Eat Me* (South Coast Rep).

Recent credits includes: *Ohio* which won The Scotsman's Fringe First Award (Edinburgh Fringe, Bristol Old Vic, Young Vic); *The Antiquities* for which Caitlin was nominated as Outstanding Director for the Drama Desk Awards (Playwrights Horizons, Vineyard Theater, Goodman Theater); *The Keep Going Song* which won the Obie Award for Sustained Achievement (LCT3); *The Good John Proctor* (Bedlam); *Find Me Here, Work Hard Have Fun Make History* (Clubbed Thumb); *Nova* (The Lyceum in Edinburgh, Pemberley); *United States vs Gupta* (JACK and New Georges); and *Sanctuary City* (New York Theatre Workshop).

Caitlin was a founding member and the Artistic Director of Seattle's critically acclaimed Satori Group and is the former Artistic Director of the Williams College Summer Theater Lab. In addition to Williams, she has worked as a teacher and director at Rutgers University, Cornish College of the Arts, Atlantic Acting School, the New School and NYU Tisch School of the Arts. She is a core faculty member at the National Theater Institute.

Born and raised in Boston, she is a graduate of Williams College, an alum of the Drama League Directors Project and Next Stage Artist Residency, a former Clubbed Thumb Directing Fellow, and a New Georges Affiliate Artist.

LYDIA COOK | Associate Director

Lydia Cook is a theatre director and maker, creating bold, playful and imaginative work that often incorporates music and movement. She is committed to amplifying underrepresented voices, including global majority, LGBTQIA+ and neurodiverse communities, sharing stories that often get overlooked. Lydia strives to make theatre accessible and engaging for everyone to experience and enjoy.

Recent Associate Director credits include: *How to Win Against History* (Bristol Old Vic, Norwich Theatre Playhouse, Edinburgh Fringe); *David Copperfield* (Theatre Royal Bath); *Emilia* (Circomedia, Bristol); and *Oliver Twist* (Tobacco Factory Theatres, Bristol).

Recent Directing credits include: *Arabella* (Hampton Court, Kensington Palace); *Holes* (Wuzhen Theatre Festival in China, Wardrobe Theatre in Bristol); *Return to the Forbidden Planet*, *Little Shop of Horrors* (The Egg, Bath); and *The Future is Beige* (Bristol Old Vic).

Lydia trained at Bristol Old Vic Theatre School, graduating with a Master's in Drama Directing.

CATE McCREA | Scenic Designer

Cate McCrea is a scenographer specializing in collaborative development of new works. Her designs are inspired by and drawn from craft techniques, recycled materials, and archival collections.

Off-Broadway credits include: The Bengsons' *Keep Going Songs* (LCT3); *The Good John Proctor* (Bedlam); *Corsicana* (Playwrights Horizons, co-design with Lael Jellinek).

Other works include: *Uncle* (The Kitchen); *Cherie Dre* (Danspace Project); *Ashkenazi Seance* (the Brick); *Let's Get Ready Together* (the Tank); *A Woman of the World* (The Acting Company); *Director Fest 2021* (Drama League at A.R.T./NY Gural Theatre); *Director Fest 2020* (Drama League at New Ohio Theatre); *Stone Belly* (Harlem Stage); and *Piramo e Tisbe* (Little Opera Theatre of New York).

Cate is part of the 2025-26 New Georges Jam and a proud member of USA 829.

DAVID BENGALI | Projection Designer

David Bengali is an award-winning projection, media, and lighting designer based in NYC.

Broadway credits include: *Water for Elephants* for which David was nominated for a Tony Award in 2024 and an Outer Critics Circle Award (Imperial Theatre); *Good Night, and Good Luck* (Winter Garden Theatre); *Eureka Day* (Manhattan Theatre Club); *The Thanksgiving Play* (Hayes Theatre); and *1776* (A.R.T., National Tour, Roundabout).

Off-Broadway credits include: *We Live in Cairo* (A.R.T, NYTW); *Here There Are Blueberries* (NYTW, La Jolla Playhouse, Signature D.C.; Hewes and Helen Hayes Awards); *Twilight: LA 1992* (Signature Theatre; Henry Hewes Award, Drama Desk Nomination); *Anthony Rapp's Without You* (New World Stages); *The Visitor* (The Public Theater; Lucille Lortel Award Nominee); *Circle Jerk* (Obie Award, Drama League Nomination); *Einstein's Dreams* (Prospect Theatre, 59E59; Drama Desk Nomination); *Van Gogh's Ear* (Signature Theatre; Drama Desk Nomination); and *The Great Leap* (Atlantic Theatre Company).

He was a 2017-2019 Arts Fellow at the Princeton University Lewis Center for the Arts and received his M.F.A. at New York University.

BETHANY GUPWELL | Lighting Designer

Bethany Gupwell is a London-based lighting designer, trained at the Royal Central School of Speech and Drama. In 2018, she was awarded the Association of Lighting Designers' Francis Reid Award.

Credits include: *All's Well That Ends Well* (Shakespeare's Globe); *Larmes de Couteat / Full Moon in March* (Royal Opera House); *Escaped Alone / What If Only, Shed: Exploded View* (Royal Exchange Theatre); *Twelfth Night, Quiet Songs, A Play for the Living in a Time of Extinction, Lay Down Your Burdens* (Barbican); *La Voix Humaine* (Opéra National du Rhin); *Dead Woman* (Schaubuhne); *Little Scratch* (Hampstead Theatre, New Diorama); *Visit from an Unknown Woman, This Much I Know, To Have and to Hold* for which Beth received an Offie nomination in 2023, *Wolf Cub* (Hampstead Theatre); *The Earthworks* (Young Vic); *Robin Hood* (Theatre Royal Bath); *Here, The Woods* (Southwark Playhouse); *Lady Dealer* (Bush Theatre); *War & Culture, Keep Watching* (New Diorama); *Ignition* (Frantic Assembly); *The Pirate, The Princess and the Platypus* (Polka Theatre); *A-Typical Rainbow* for which Beth received an Offie nomination in 2022 (Turbine); *In Praise Of Love, Rice, Little Baby Jesus* (Orange Tree); *Little Brother, Brown Girls Do It Too: Mama Told Me Not to Come, Fitter, Wonder Winterland* (Soho Theatre); *Talking Heads* (Watford Palace).

NICK KOURTIDES | Sound Designer

Nick Kourtides designs for musical theatre and creates sound environments for devised ensemble works. He is the global sound designer for *Magic Mike Live* in Las Vegas, London, Berlin, and Australia.

Off-Broadway Credits Include: O*ratorio for Living Things* (Signature, Ars Nova); *Three Houses* (Signature); *The Keep Going Songs* (LCT3); *Travels, The Lucky Ones* (Ars Nova); *Heather Christian's Terce* (Prototype Theatre); *Blacklight* (Greenwich House); *Object Lesson* (NYTW, BAM); *Elephant Room* (St. Ann's Warehouse); *Carson McCullers Talks About Love* (Rattlestick); and *Jomama Jones: Radiate* (Soho Rep).

Regional Credits Include: *Macbeth in Stride* for Shakespeare Theatre and Philadelphia Theatre Company (Yale Repertory Theatre, BAM Harvey Theater, Michael R. Klein Theatre, Suzanne Roberts Theatre); *Lady Day at Emerson's Bar and Grill* (Actors Theatre of Louisville); *You're a Good Man, Charlie Brown* (Cincinnati Playhouse in the Park); *The Waves* for New York Stage and Film (The Hallie Flanagan Davis Powerhouse Theater); *The Mousetrap* (McCarter Theatre Center); *The Lonely Few* (Geffen Playhouse); *The Comedy of Errors* (Folger Theatre); *If I Forget* (Studio Theatre); *Next to Normal* (Milwaukee Rep); *Passing Strange* (The Wilma Theatre); *The 25th Annual Putnam County Spelling Bee* for Philadelphia Theatre Company (Suzanne Roberts Theatre, Paper Mill Playhouse); and *Dreamgirls, Anyone Can Whistle* (Prince Music Theater).

With Pig Iron Theatre Company: *A Period of Animate Existence*; *Cankerblossom*; *Isabella*; *Chekhov Lizardbrain*, und *Mission to Mercury*.

With Rainpan43 at the Edinburgh Festival Fringe: *Object Lesson* (Summerhall); *Elephant Room* (Assembly); and *Flesh and Blood & Fish and Fowl* (Traverse).

Nick has taught Sound Design for Live Performance at Drexel University and Swarthmore College. He has received an Obie, Lucille Lortel, Bessie, and Barrymore awards.

www.nickkourtides.com

CECI CALF | Associate Scenic Designer

Ceci is a set and costume designer based in London. She trained at The Royal Welsh College of Music and Drama and has since worked across the UK and Europe.

Upcoming productions include *Emma* directed by Stephen Unwin (Theatre Royal Bath, UK Tour).

Recent credits include: *Comedy of Errors* (Shakespeare Theatre Company, Washington); *Don Giovanni, The Barber of Seville* (Waterperry Festival Opera); *HIR* starring Felicity Huffman, *Our Cosmic Dust* (Park Theatre); *Stiletto: The Musical* (Charing Cross Theatre); *Farm Hall* (Jermyn Street,

Theatre Royal Bath, UK Tour, West End); *Autobiography of a Cad, Much Ado About Nothing, Othello* (Watermill Theatre, Newbury); *A Christmas Carol* (Opera Holland Park, Concert); *The Ritual Slaughter of Gorge Mastromas, A Skull In Connemara* (Dailes Teātris Riga in Latvia); *Under The Black Rock* (Arcola); *Breeding* (Kings Head Theatre); *Warrior Queens* (Sadler's Wells); *Waiting For Anya, The Mozart Question* (Barn Theatre); *One Million Tiny Plays About Britain* for which Ceci was Nominated for an Offie Award: Best Set Design (Jermyn Street, Watermill Theatre); *Yes So I Said Yes* for which Ceci Won the Standing Ovation Award: Best Production and was Nominated for an Offie Award: Set Design, *How To Survive An Apocalypse, Not Quite Jerusalem* and *The Wind of Heaven* for which Ceci won the Standing Ovation award: Best Rediscovery/Adaptation (Finborough Theatre).

Associate credits: *A Streetcar Named Desire* (Sheffield Crucible); *Macbeth* starring Ralph Fiennes, *Anything Is Possible If You Think About It Hard Enough* (Southwark Playhouse).

www.cecicalf.com

OSCAR BURR | Associate Lighting Designer & Programmer

Recent credits include: *The Maladies* (Kiln Theatre); *Show Pony* (UK Tour); *Queen of Wands* (Union Theatre); *A Christmas Carol(Ish)* (Soho Place); *Bad Road* (Union Theatre); *The Dreams of A Ridiculous Man* (Marylebone Theatre).

DAN SAMSON | Associate Sound Designer

Sound Design includes: *Percy Jackson and The Lightning Thief* (UK Tour); *How to Win Against History* (Bristol Old Vic, Norwich Theatre Playhouse, Edinburgh); *Heathers* (New York, @Soho Place London, Theatre Royal Haymarket, UK Tour, The Other Palace); *Grease* (Germany, Austria, Switzerland Tour); *Filumena* (UK Tour); *Abenteuerland Das Musical* (Capitol Theatre Düsseldorf); *Calendar Girl* (UK Tour); *Kathy and Stella Solve A Murder!* (West End, Edinburgh Festival, UK Tour); *Berlusconi The Musical* (Southwark Playhouse Elephant); *The Famous Five* (Theatre Clwyd, Chichester Festival Theatre); *Fisherman's Friends The Musical* (Hall for Cornwall, UK Tour, Canada); *The Cher Show* (UK Tour); *The Osmonds* (UK Tour); *Love Letters* (Theatre Royal Haymarket); *Berlin Berlin* (German Tour); *Saturday Night Fever* (UK Tour); *Cilla The Musical* (UK Tour); *Ghost* (UK Tour, International Tour, Paris Mogador, Moscow MDM); *Rain Man* (UK Tour); *Rough Crossing* (UK Tour); *Cabaret* (UK Tour); *La Cage aux Folles* (UK Tour); *Evita* (Dominion, Phoenix, UK and International Tour); *How the Other Half Loves* (Theatre Royal Haymarket, Duke of York's, UK Tour); *Save The Last Dance For Me* (UK Tour); *Dreamboats and Petticoats* (UK Tour); *The War of The Worlds* (Dominion); *Rehearsal for Murder* (UK Tour); *Sinatra On Stage* (The London Palladium); *The Glenn Miller Story* (London Coliseum, UK Tour); *The Sound of*

Music (UK Tour); *Jesus Christ Superstar* (UK Tour); *Blood Brothers* (UK Tour); *Joseph and the Amazing Technicolour Dreamcoat* (Newcastle Arena, UK Tour); *Dreamboats and Miniskirts* (UK Tour); *Ain't Misbehavin'* (Colchester Mercury, Southwark Playhouse); and *Carrie* (Southwark Playhouse).

ALISON KOPIT | Access Dramaturg

Alison Kopit is a queer and disabled cultural worker, access dramaturg, and movement artist based between Chicago and New York City. She was awarded the Michael Feingold award for Dramaturgy in the 2023 Obie Awards and holds a PhD in Disability Studies from the University of Illinois at Chicago.

Alison has been creating and developing an access dramaturgy practice with her collaborators that approaches access as central to the full creative process, and integrates access creatively into all levels of a production. She began to hone this practice with Ryan J. Haddad's Obie Award winning *Dark Disabled Stories* during the Spring of 2023, produced by the Bushwick Starr and The Public Theater, presented by The Public Theater, dir. Jordan Fein.

She was honored and thrilled to further explore access dramaturgy with the brilliant team of *Ohio* by The Bengsons.

Other recent access dramaturgy collaborations include: *Radiate* (Red Eye Theater); *Hold Me in the Wuter* (Playwrights Horizons); *Air Change Per Hour* (Issue Project Room); and *Dan Fishback is Alive, Unwell & Living in His Apartment* (Joe's Pub).

Alison is a co-director of the Pay Rate for Access Workers Now (PRAWN) project with Madison Zalopany, which advocates for greater standards of pay for access workers through research and consultation with cultural spaces. She also provides training and consultation to cultural spaces that want to grow in their access-centered practices and connections to the disability community.

www.alisonkopit.com

JACK BOISSIEUX PRODUCTION MANAGEMENT | Production Manager

JBPM is a production management company, working across theatre, opera, dance, musicals and events. They have worked on national and international touring productions, West End musicals and immersive/site specific theatre. Alongside a range of productions with Francesca Moody Productions over the last couple of years, JBPM have production managed a variety of projects.

Recent and current credits include: *The Choir Of Man* (West End, European and International Touring); *Bluey's Big Play* (European and International Touring); Waterperry Opera Festival 2021-2024; *Pied Piper* (National Touring);

The Ancient Oak Of Baldor (National Touring); *A Very Naughty Christmas* (Southwark Playhouse, Elephant); *Wilko* (Queen's Theatre Hornchurch); *Lay Down Your Burdens* (Barbican and National Touring); *Lavender, Hyacinth, Violet, Yew* (Bush Theatre); *Lost Lending Library and A Curious Quest* (Punchdrunk); *Maddie Moate's Very Curious Christmas* (Apollo Theatre).

FMP is an Olivier Award-winning, Tony nominated production company whose work in theatre has originated two of the most globally successful television shows of the last decade: *Fleabag* and *Baby Reindeer*.

We make original theatre, television, film, audio and live events. We believe in finding the right home for the right story and growing it over time. From tiny fringe theatres to the West End, to the next big Amazon television series and beyond.

We're serious about our work, but we don't take ourselves too seriously. We work with leading writers and nurture new talent to produce bold, award-winning shows with huge potential and something to say – be it drama, comedy, horror, or musicals. Our work is itch-scratching, big-swinging and full of heart.

Current & upcoming productions: *Weather Girl* (St Ann's Warehouse); *Ohio* (Young Vic, Assembly Roxy, Bristol Old Vic); *Relics* (Lyric Hammersmith); *Feeling Afraid As If Something Terrible Is Going To Happen* (Studio Theatre, Washington DC).

Recent productions include: Shedinburgh Fringe Festival; *My Master Builder* (Wyndham's Theatre); *An Oak Tree* (Young Vic, Bergen International Festival, Festival d'Avignon, Royal Lyceum Theatre Edinburgh); *How to Win Against History* (Bristol Old Vic, Norwich Theatre Playhouse, Underbelly); *Garry Starr: Classic Penguins* (Soho Theatre, Underbelly); *A Streetcar Named Desire* (Noël Coward Theatre, BAM, Phoenix Theatre); *Kathy and Stella Solve a Murder* (The Ambassadors Theatre, Underbelly Edinburgh, Bristol Old Vic, HOME Manchester, Roundabout); *Weather Girl* (Soho Theatre, Summerhall); *Feeling Afraid As If Something Terrible is Going to Happen* (Arts Centre Melbourne, Sydney Opera House, Adelaide Fringe Festival, Bush Theatre, Roundabout); *I'm Almost There* (Summerhall); *VL* (Roundabout); *Nutcracker* (Southbank Centre); *Never Have I Ever* (Chichester Festival Theatre); *School Girls; Or, The African Mean Girls Play* (Lyric Hammersmith); *A Doll's House* (Hudson Theatre, New York); *Lemons Lemons Lemons Lemons Lemons* (Harold Pinter Theatre); *Berlusconi: A New Musical* (Southwark Playhouse Elephant); *Mum* (Soho Theatre); *Leopards* (Rose Theatre); *Baby Reindeer* (Bush Theatre, Roundabout); and *Fleabag* (Wyndham's Theatre, Soho Playhouse, Soho Theatre, UK and Australian Tour, S.Korea, Underbelly).

Executive Producer: Francesca Moody
Shedinburgh Producer: Darcy Dobson
Associate Producer: Grace Dickson
Shedinburgh Assistant Producer: Tom Chamberlain
Production Coordinator: Rory Thomas-Howes
Production Assistant: Angel Mika Kemp
Creative Associate: Jon Brittain
Production Associate: Jack Boissieux

www.francescamoody.com

piece by piece productions

piece by piece productions was founded by Wendy vanden Heuvel in 1999 as an independent creative production company based in New York and California. Along with executive producers, Kendra Bator and Tom Casserly, piece by piece has co-produced productions with Rattlestick Playwrights Theater, Mabou Mines, St Ann's Warehouse, Z Space, The Wooster Group, A.C.T, and the Under the Radar Festival.

Notable productions include: *Medea* which won the Evening Standard Award for Best Actress (Fiona Shaw) and Best Director (Deborah Warner) (Brooks Atkinson Theatre on Broadway); *My Name is Rachel Corrie* (Minetta Lane Theatre); *Elective Affinities* by David Adjmi with Zoe Caldwell (a unique site-specific event at an Upper East Side townhouse in New York City); *The Tricky Part* by Martin Moran which won a 2004 Obie award and two Drama Desk nominations including Outstanding Play (The Barrow Group, The McGinn-Cazale Theater); The Bengsons' *Hundred Days* which won the The Bay Area Outstanding New Musical in 2014 (Z Space); The Bengsons' *The Lucky Ones* (Ars Nova, 2018); *The Lake Lucille Chekhov Project* (*Ivanov, Seagull, Cherry Orchard*) co-produced with co-founders Brian Mertes and Melissa Kievman.

piece by piece commissioned and developed the Bengsons' *Ohio* and co-produced developmental productions in 2021 with St. Ann's Warehouse and in 2023 with the Actors Theatre of Louisville.

In 2024-2025, piece by piece produced *A Knock on the Roof* by Khawla Ibraheem, directed by Oliver Butler; it was presented at the Edinburgh Fringe, where it received widespread acclaim and won the Scotsman Fringe First Award. Afterwards, it toured to Dublin Theatre Festival, New York Theatre Workshop/UTR and the Royal Court Theatre.

Film credits include: *The Rest I Make Up* (2018, Directed by Michelle Memran).

Young Vic

Founded in 1970 as a space for world-premiere productions and unexpected takes on classic plays, the Young Vic has been one of London's leading theatres for more than fifty years.

Welcoming 100,000 visitors a year, the Young Vic stands out in the nation's cultural landscape for balancing daring commercial drive and artistic flair with genuine grassroots social impact work within our community. This success is seen most vividly in the audience group for which we are famous; the most diverse, lively and engaged in London. This is the fruit of years of building involvement among local young people. We forge deep connections in our neighbourhood through our Taking Part programme, where we engage with over 15,000 people every year via a wide range of projects, from skills-based workshops to on-stage performances.

We believe great art belongs to everyone. Ticket prices are kept low no matter how high the demand and 10% of tickets are given free within the local community; enabling a unique, no-risk taste of great theatre for thousands of people.

Our unique, fully flexible auditoria allows us to present great plays by and with the next generation of theatre artists alongside work by some of the world's great directors, actors and designers. We are proud to be a Director's Theatre known for launching careers and a combination of youth and genius which makes us one of the most vibrant theatres in the UK.

Built upon the principles of access, innovation, and community, the Young Vic is deepening its roots nationally and internationally. Recent transfers include *Punch*, *Best of Enemies* and *Oklahoma!* in the West End and *Death of a Salesman* and *The Collaboration* on Broadway.

Some theatres present great plays. Some give young artists opportunities to grow. Some build strong and lasting relationships with their community. The Young Vic does all three.

Artistic Director: **Nadia Fall**
Executive Director: **Lucy Pattison**

Public Support:

Production Support:

SUPPORTED BY
THE SEASON CIRCLE

Young Vic Staff

Board of Directors
Glenn Earle
Nicky Dunn OBE
Robert Easton
Farah Ramza Golant CBE
Ali Hossaini
Andrea Ling
Joshua Parr
Fiona Shaw
Kobna Holdbrook-Smith MBE
Anna Williams

Executive
Nadia Fall – Artistic Director
Lucy Pattison – Executive Director
Emily Ansorge – Executive Assistant

Artistic
Jack Bradley – Artistic Associate
Lisa Makin – Artistic Associate
Sean Brooks – Senior Producer
Emily Hamilton – Assistant Producer

Creators' Program
Sylvian Cunningham – Creators' Program Coordinator

Development
Gemma Cook – Development Director
Georgie Neve – Head of Philanthropy
Maggie Fowles – Grants Partnerships Manager
Layla Moosavi Rivers – Corporate Partnerships Manager
Anouk Smith – Memberships & Campaigns Officer
Mairin Schmidt – Development & Events Coordinator

Finance
Orla Sanders – Head of Finance
Amy Morbin – Finance Coordinator

Marketing & Audiences
Beatrice Burrows – Director of Marketing & Audiences
Su-Ann Chow-Seegoolam – Head of Press & Communications
Zoe Fitzpatrick – Senior Ticketing & Sales Manager
Rebecca Jeetoo – Senior Marketing Manager
Beth Golison – Social Media & Digital Content Manager
Aimee Dickinson – Digital Marketing & Campaigns Officer
Bread and Butter PR – Press Support

People
Maria Khan – Director of People
Jennifer Horan – People Coordinator

Operations
Harvey Dhadda – Head of Theatre Operations
Max Puplett – Deputy Head of Theatre Operations
Eleanor Kumar – Front of House Manager
Kitti Wells – Trainee Facilities Manager
Damilola Senbanjo – Digital Systems Analyst

Production Staff
Kat Ellis – Technical Director
Carmel Macaree – Deputy Production Manager
Claire Stamp – Head of Sound
Rhodri Sion Evans – Head of Stage
Aimee Russam – Head of Costume
Faye Hetherington – Head of Lighting
Neil McKeown – Deputy Head of Sound
Aaron Storey – Deputy Head of Stage
Maddie Bevan – Deputy Head of Costume
Georgina Heaton – Deputy Head of Lighting
Rachel MacLoughlin – Workshop Manager
Harry Leng Bloodworth – Stage and Workshop Technician
Luke Jackson – Lighting Technician

Taking Part
Melanie Anouf – Learning Producer
Aaliyah Antoine – Participation Producer
Alisha Artry – Neighbourhood Theatre Producer
Michelle Cullimore – Taking Part Coordinator

Welcome Team
Joel Oladapo – Stage Door & Welcome Team
Lauren Holden – Duty Manager (Casual)
Sarah Berryman – Duty Manager (Casual)
Sebastian Houilon – Duty Manager (Casual)
Eimear Griffin – Welcome Team
Tia Harding – Welcome Team
Edward Jones – Welcome Team
Chris Stevens – Welcome Team (Casual)
Kathy Bolt – Welcome Team (Casual)

Ushers
Aisha Edwards – Usher
Alicia Pope – Usher
Amy Rushent – Usher
Andre Da Silva-Jenkins – Usher
Athansie Munyaneza – Usher
Benjamin Clarke – Usher
Carla Cuscito – Usher
Cassiopeia Berkeley-Agyepong – Usher
Charlotte Micalef – Usher
Chenta Shayen Marigueo – Usher
Chiara Lari – Usher
Ciaran Cross – Usher
Daniel Nash – Usher
Daniella Connor – Usher
Debbie Burningham – Usher
Eboni Dixon – Usher
Eleanor Sandover – Usher
Elijah Bangura – Usher
Elliot Woods – Usher
Ellis Jupiter – Usher
Erin Thomas – Usher
Francesca Cary – Usher
Grace Kayibanda – Usher
Gracjana Rejmer-Canovas – Usher
Hana Jennings – Usher
Harrison Evans – Usher
Henry Thorpe-Spinks – Usher
Isaac Vincent – Usher
Isabel Stone – Usher
James Sparkes – Usher
Jasmine Silk – Usher
Jida Akil – Usher
Joanna Selcott – Usher
Josh Hitchman-Pinnock – Usher
Joyce Clark – Usher
Julie Patten – Usher
Kate Gambold – Usher
Lanikai Krishnadasan Torrens – Usher
Liam Thorley – Usher
Lilly Conley – Usher
Linden Sloan – Usher
Lynn Knight – Usher
Matheus Vianna – Usher
Megan Vernon – Usher
Michael Hawkins – Usher
Nastassja Dao – Usher
Natalie Bott – Usher
Oliver Byng – Usher
Paula Shaw – Usher
Pearl Adams – Usher
Phoebe Bakker – Usher
Priscilla Boateng – Usher
Rohan Dhupar – Usher
Shanti Esnard Echanove – Usher
Sharitah Boulton – Usher
Sherifat Bakare – Usher
Simone Bell – Usher
Starr Ballard – Usher
Tanjiana Bryan-Hesse – Usher
Tramo Gillespie – Usher
Urielle Klein- Mekongo – Usher
William Lewis – Usher

Our Supporters

The Young Vic relies on the generous support of many individuals, trusts and foundations, and companies to produce our work, on stage and in our community. For their recent support, we thank:

2025 Inaugural Season Supporters
Glenn Earle
Patrick Handley
Phil & Sarah Mohr
Olwyn Foundation
Rosalind Riley
Sarina Taylor

Production Supporters
The Charlotte Aitken Trust

Major Donors
Robert Easton & Elza Blankenburgs
Linda Keenan
Clive Lewis
Sarah & Dominic Murphy

Philanthropic Supporters
Pembe Al Mazrouei
Neil & Sarah Brener
Dorothy Chou
Lord Mervyn & Lady Jeanne Davies
Kene & Ifeoma Ejikeme
Manfred & Lydia Gorvy
Victoria Greenwood & Lionel Barber
Sophie Hale & Roland Rudd
Frances Hellman & Warren Breslau
The Ilube Family
Adam Kenwright
The McLain Foundation

Soul Mates
Nicola Arkell Reed
Chris & Frances Bates
Katie Bradford
CJ & LM Braithwaite
Jim Carroll
Fatma Charlwood
Tim & Caroline Clark
Caroline Clasen
James & Victoria Corcoran
Lin & Ken Craig
David desJardins
Robyn Durie
Jennifer & Jeff Eldredge
Dermot Finch
Emily Fletcher
Sue Fletcher
Tim Fosberry & Joseph Mubiru
Frankie Greenall
Elizabeth Griffith
Julie Grigg
Alan & Ros Haigh
Patricia Hamzahee
Madeleine Hodgkin
Nik Holttum & Helen Brannigan
Samantha Huggins
Peter Hughes
Melanie J. Johnson
David Kaskel & Christopher Teano
Nicola Kerr
Naveen Kler
Sybil Kretzmer
Ann Lewis
Frances Lynn
Ian McKellen
Gary Morris
Brian & Meredith Niles
Katherine Norman
Barbara Reeves
Corinne Rooney
Sir Paul & Lady Ruddock CBE
Marion Schoenfeld
Dr Bhagat Sharma
Jenny Sheridan
Professor Wendy Sigle
Michael Silton & Susan Myer Silton
Ilina Singh
Marjorie Smith
Clare Stirzaker
Jan & Michael Topham
Brian Turner
Robert & Gillian Wallace
Funmi Watson
Alice Whitaker
Dagny & Ryad Yousuf

With thanks to our Friends and Good Friends not listed above, and to all our supporters who wish to remain anonymous

Major Trusts & Foundations
Anonymous
Backstage Trust
The Charlotte Aitken Trust
Jerwood Foundation

Trusts & Foundations
The Andor Charitable Trust
The Austin & Hope Pilkington Trust
The Childhood Trust
Cleopatra Trust
The D'Oyly Carte Charitable Trust
The John S Cohen Foundation
The John Thaw Foundation
Maria Björnson Memorial Fund
The Martin Bowley Charitable Trust
The Noël Coward Foundation
Royal Victoria Hall Foundation
The Thompson Family Charitable Trust

Corporate Members
Anonymous
Bank of America
Bloomberg
FGS Global

Hotel Partner
Bankside Hotel, Autograph Collection

Media Partner
OMD UK

Legacy Supporters
Ian Burford & Alec Cannell
Sheila Maureen Harvey Estate
The Midgley family, donated by Jenny Marshall

Development Board
Sarah Thorpe Scott (Chair)
Toccara Baker
Nicky Black
Dorothy Chou
Dermot Finch
Sophie Hale
Phil Mohr
Barbara Reeves
Julia Zilberman

OHIO

The Bengsons

Characters

SHAUN
ABIGAIL

This text went to press before the end of rehearsals and so may differ slightly from the play as performed.

Soundcheck.

SHAUN & ABIGAIL. Hello! WELCOME!

ABIGAIL. Can you hear me?

Soundchecking mics.

SHAUN. Can you hear this?

Soundchecking instruments.

Can you see this?

Checking captions.

ABIGAIL. If you can hear this, sing it back to me.

ABIGAIL *sings a tone.*

ABIGAIL *builds a simple chord – Hey eh hey – and also loops it eventually with the audience, which* SHAUN *quickly helps to transform into a groove which lifts until:*

The tone becomes a loop.

(*Over loop.*) This is a death concert!
Shaun's gonna die at the end!

SHAUN. Yay.

ABIGAIL. We're so excited to be here!

ABIGAIL *stops the audience's clapping.*

When our son Louie was three, I was lying in bed with him and I was trying to get him to sleep.
And he looked at me and said, 'How long am I going to be able to do any of this?'
I said, 'What do you mean?'
He said, 'What happens when we die?'
And I wasn't ready for the question
So I panicked, and I told him the truth as I understood it in that moment that:

Music stops.

our bodies turn to muck and we are eaten by worms.

Music resumes.

And he cried. He cried so hard.

SHAUN. So sensitive…

ABIGAIL. So I just started whipping through all the world religions, just like, everybody's best ideas so far.
I said, 'Well maybe our bodies are star stuff – the minerals in our bodies are made from the explosions of stars long ago, and when we die, we will dissolve and the minerals in our bodies go back into other living things like apples and herons and cardinals and frogs…'
And he hated that.

SHAUN. He did not like that.

ABIGAIL. So then I went to reincarnation. Because at least then we would be *people.* I said, 'So maybe you will be a little boy again, and I will be a mommy again and we'll find each other…'
And he said, 'Find each other WHERE?'

SHAUN. Like, the logistics were a nightmare.

ABIGAIL. And so finally…

My baby is crying, it's late at night, and I was tired. So I succumbed. To heaven.

Music becomes a tone.

And I said, 'Okay honey, there's this place, and when we die, we all go there. And it's perfect. And when we go there, we are unchanged, in fact we're like, peak fitness… You will be exactly you, and I will be exactly me, and I will go there first and I will wait for you.'
And he fell sweetly to sleep.

Music out.

SHAUN. So
   You know
   We lied.

The 'Hey' loop comes back in, more clapping.

ABIGAIL. So Shaun and I are both disabled, we'll hold for applause.

Our situations are degenerative and we've been mostly bummed about this.
A lot of shame, a lot of fear, mostly because it's new, and you know, change is for chumps.

Also coming into disability means leaning on community – yuck!

SHAUN. Gross.

ABIGAIL. And death!
Our disabilities remind us we're gonna die someday. So!

We're doing this to try to get less afraid. Of change. Community. And most of all death.

SHAUN. I come from a long line of people who believed in heaven. Pastors, organists, deacons. What's a deacon?

When I was a child I believed in heaven. I threw that away whole hog and now when my kid is scared I have nothing to comfort him with except lies.

I loved believing in heaven. Everything solved. But even then I was also unsatisfied. I could feel there was something... something more? Something less?

Okay, so! Let's do this.

When *I* was three years old
I was walking along one of the wild shallow creeks of Ohio which are full of the fossils of ancient sea creatures and Coors Light beer cans.

The sound of cicadas.

This was the eighties so I was unsupervised.

ABIGAIL *sings.*

And happy! Singing *The Care Bears* theme song.
Listening to the creek and to the cicadas. The water was shallow, just up to my ankles.

And then the next step –
I was thrust into this new plane of existence where everything I knew was gone and all things and all time exist as one. By which I mean –

SHAUN *stops the sounds.*

I died

Sinkhole sounds – water swirling and rumbling.

Muddy water was filling my mouth my eyes my ears
It swallowed me
I'd fallen into a sinkhole.
A narrow, six-foot hole in the middle of the creek.

ABIGAIL *builds the 'Requiem' loop.*

The water is way over my head, spiraling into my ears.
I couldn't swim.
I could taste… sweet clay, decaying plant matter.
And then a sound I can recognize. My cicadas.

And my whole body just went limp.
And maybe this isn't so bad
Maybe I can follow this new sound inside the labyrinth of my own ear
and become a turtle a heron a brand new little boy and
I'm not ready for this I'm not ready for this
Then hands pull me up

The sinkhole sounds stop. ABIGAIL *begins to hum.*

And my father is singing to me to calm me down
And though my ears were ringing with death
or perhaps light lead poisoning from the river that had famously caught fire only a few years before.

I could hear my father

And he whispered God into my ear

ABIGAIL. We're going to ask for your help tonight, we figure you can learn all your parts this time and then come back another day and nail it. For today, we're in it together. We're standing on a map of Ohio. Just north of Ohio is Canada! Is there anyone here from Canada? Been to Canada?

Know of Canada? Okay, when I point to you I need you to
sing 'OH CANADA'. Let's practice! 'OH CANADA!'
So if this is Ohio
You're in Indiana
You're in Kentucky… you may wanna get out.
You're in West Virginia, regular Virginia, Mexico is up the
stairs… and Nicaragua is across the Themes.
Okay anyone here speak a little Spanish? Or any language
other than English? Okay when I ask you to, I need you to
pray in that language. OR! If prayers aren't for you, you could
like, order a cheeseburger or something, we'll never know.
So Shaun and I are autistic, we stim a lot, you are also
welcome to do whatever is right for your body all night
and for the entire rest of your lives. And, if you're able
and willing, we'd love for you to keep time with us in a
moment – stamp a foot or whatever. Okay. I think we're
ready.

SHAUN. So, there I am, in my father's arms.
I believed everything then, and I could hear everything, too.
I could hear the rumble of the generator trying to kick on all
night in the trailer next door,

A low thumping beat.

ABIGAIL *invites the audience to stamp their feet.*

I could hear the murmur of voices praying in English and in
Spanish.
And I could hear the loud polyphonic roar of the insects in
the field.

A wide resonant humming – an ancient sound.

Throat singing – ABIGAIL *invites song – the sound of the
ancestors and the wild gods.*

SUMMER SUMMER
(*humming with a joyful incantation on top*)

OH SUMMER SUMMER FATHER MOTHER
  MOTHER FATHER
GRASSES GROWING TALLER
LIFE DOWN IN THE HOLLER
OH

> HOLDING ON TO BOTH THEIR KNEES US LOVING JESUS
> OH I LOVE MY MOTHER, OH I LOVE MY FATHER
> CALLING ALL MY PEOPLE
> ANGELS IN THE STEEPLE
> FATHER YOU ADORE US WE WILL SING THE CHORUS
> WE WILL SING THE CHORUS, OOO
> EVERYWHERE I GO IS YOU
> THE BODY OF THE WORLD IS MADE OF YOU

(*Spoken.*) I am three years old. Winnie the Pooh and Jesus Christ both died for me bloodily upon the cross. We are living on a Christian commune in the wooded hills of Ohio, called Jubilee. We are crammed in four families to a trailer and our yogurt is home-made! My father is eight feet tall and his shorts are shorter than mine, his mustache is a thicket reaching to the heavens. He is a pastor and one day I wanna grow up and be a pastor just like him. Like his upstretched arms we pray

SHAUN & ABIGAIL AS JOHN.
> OH
> SPRING AND SUMMER
> SUMMER IN THE WATER
> WATCH OUT FOR THE MOCCASINS
> SLIPPING IN THE RAPIDS

ABIGAIL AS JOHN.
> HOLD ON TO YOUR HAT KID

SHAUN.
> OH
> I WAS JUST A BOY OF THREE OR FOUR
> I WAS REACHING FOR THE PRUNE JAR
> THERE WAS NOTHING SWEETER
> ANGELS IN THE STEEPLE
> UP OUT OF THE FOREST
> BIRDS WOULD SING THE CHORUS
> BIRDS WOULD SING THE CHORUS OOO
> I WAS SURE THE FOREST OOO
> I WAS SURE THE FOREST HELD ME TRUE

(*Spoken.*) It is the mid-eighties and there are all these terrible civil wars happening down in Central America. And they are all being low-key started and funded by the CIA. So our government isn't accepting refugees… but Canada is.

OH CANADA! chorus.

So we here in Jubilee, we drive busses down to the border, we scoop up refugees, take them back across the Ohio river, which was the freedom line for the underground railroad, teach them English on our commune and then get them into Canada.

OH CANADA!

My father flies to Nicaragua
Where he meets with both the government and the contras
He knows this is what he was born to do
The travel, the activism.

SHAUN & ABIGAIL. Praying in English!
Praying in Spanish!

ABIGAIL. Pray! Order your cheeseburgers!

The audience prays in various languages.

SHAUN. My father is the exact age I am now
It is Easter Sunday in 1986
He leads us in prayer and he sounds like this:

ABIGAIL.
OHH
SPRING AND SUMMER CALLING ALL MY SISTER BROTHERS
BABIES SLEEPING LAMBS ARE LEAPING
OH
JESUS DIES AND CHRIST ARISEN
HE IS CHOSEN WE ARE GIVEN
SWEETNESS AND HONEY

ABIGAIL & SHAUN.
HOLY WATER
LORD AND FATHER
OH THERE IS A JOYFUL NOISE THAT RINGS FROM

> EVERYTHING THAT YOU CAN SEE
> EVERYTHING THAT YOU CAN SEE, SHAUN
> EVERY SINGLE THING THAT YOU CAN SEE

ABIGAIL *goes to set up a miniature living room.*

SHAUN. When I was a little boy, on the commune, God was not abstract. He was this very real, physical presence in my life. Kinda like a family member, like Uncle God. Like 'Did you call Uncle God? It's his birthday.'

ABIGAIL. Which is Christmas.

SHAUN. So when my dad got called up to be the pastor of this church in a conservative suburb
I thought God would come with us.
And… he did? But when we got there he was different.
He was… a little judgmental.
Still always there
But more like a stern ghost watching you masturbate.
Real racist grandpa energy.
This is also when I found out about hell, and how everyone was going there. Except hopefully us!
So, in response, we all got haircuts. We took showers, every single day! We got our polos and our khakis and this was the nineties so you know they were ill-fitting.

ABIGAIL *makes a tone.*

ABIGAIL. Can you hear this?

SHAUN. Oh! Now I need to tell you that I'm losing my hearing!
Yes I can hear that.
My father gave me two gifts
One, this glorious Jesus is a zombie superhero faith tradition
And two, congenital degenerative hearing loss
My family is full of pastors who have lost their hearing.

ABIGAIL *makes a tone.*

ABIGAIL. Can you hear this?

SHAUN. Yes
My dad was a pastor he isn't one anymore.

ABIGAIL. Can you hear this?

ABIGAIL *makes a tone.*

SHAUN. No?
His hearing is mostly gone now

ABIGAIL *makes a tone.*

No?

So you may be wondering: Is this a story about how you should feel bad for me about my ears? Absolutely not.
Do I wake in the night full of sorrow and despair? Absolutely.
Am I going to turn into my father?
What's with all these questions. Leave me alone, London.
When I was a kid, I could hear everything.

And by the time I was a teenager, in a living room very much like this one

Pointing to the miniature.

I couldn't anymore.

ABIGAIL *makes a tone.*

No.

ABIGAIL *makes a tone.*

No.

ABIGAIL *makes a tone.*

No.

ABIGAIL *playing piano, a light melancholy pattern.*

VOICES

WITH MY FRIENDS IN THE SUMMER WE'D TURN
UP THE AMPS
THEN WE'D LIE IN THE DRIVEWAY AS MY EARS
RING

WITH MY KNEES ON THE KNEELER AND MY
ARMS ON THE PEW
MY EARS ARE RINGING, I DON'T HEAR YOU

WHEN DID I STOP HEARING CICADAS IN THE
   BOWER OF THE GARDEN
BY THE RESERVOIR

IN MY BED AT NIGHT I LIE THERE READING
I KNOW THAT I AM BREATHING
BUT MY EARS COULDN'T HEAR MY BREATH AT
   ALL
PUT MY HAND ON MY CHEST
TO FEEL THE RISE AND FALL

IN THE SUMMER IN THE HONDA ON THE WAY TO
   CHURCH
I HEAR THE SOUND OF THE BUGS ON THE
   WINDSHIELD
MY FATHER DOESN'T CATCH MY VOICE
AS WE PASS THE OLD CORNFIELDS

I CAN TELL BY HIS FACE THAT HE HASN'T
   HEARD
IT HAPPENS ALL THE TIME NOW
I WATCH MY FATHER PREACH THE HOLY WORD
FROM THE ALTAR AND UNDERNEATH THE PINE
   BOUGH

IN MY BED AT NIGHT I LIE THERE READING
I KNOW THAT I AM BREATHING
BUT MY EARS COULDN'T HEAR MY BREATH AT
   ALL
PUT MY HAND ON MY CHEST
TO FEEL THE RISE AND FALL

ABIGAIL *singing wordlessly underneath.*

THERE ARE VOICES IN OHIO
THAT I USED TO HEAR
THERE ARE VOICES IN OHIO

THERE ARE VOICES IN OHIO
THAT I USED TO HEAR
THERE ARE VOICES IN OHIO

AHH

SHAUN *takes off his guitar, takes his mic to the miniature.*

This is a loving recreation of the living rooms of my people.
In these rooms, we don't speak.
I've been told the Brits might relate to this.
We go to church every Sunday, and church is quiet. And then every Sunday *after* church, we'd sit in a circle in a living room very much like this one, with our plates of jello salad – In complete silence!
Just giving you some back story on Lutherans.
Now, I was new, and the other kids would whisper… something to me? A key that could have unlocked this whole new society? And I couldn't understand them. Physically I couldn't. Not helping matters, I was also deeply weird. So they tried two, three times and then they kind of gave up, and I was alone.
I never ever spoke.
The only time I could open my mouth was when I was singing. To myself. Also alone.
But there was one person who heard me. Our choir director, Mrs Kay Wean.

ABIGAIL. So now we need you to be Mrs Wean. The captions are also going to become your teleprompter. You'll have some lines up there, okay, prep thyself.

SHAUN. She gets me to join the choir.
So I'm huddled way in the back
When she locks eyes with me, like laser beams

MRS WEAN. Hey. You.

SHAUN. She grabs me by the back of my collar and pulls me to the front

MRS WEAN. Come here right this minute.

SHAUN. I try to shrink inside my body, like fold in on myself like a black hole

MRS WEAN. Excuse me MR BENGSON – I SEE YOU. AND!

Church organ begins the melody.

SHAUN (*over the preceding music*). And I'm like
Oh she's looking at me

Oh gosh
It's getting closer
I can't do this!

MRS WEAN. MR BENGSON – THIS IS YOUR SOLO.

SHAUN. I cannot!

MRS WEAN. NOW!

SHAUN. No no no no no no no no

Straight into…

> HOLY, HOLY, HOLY!
> MERCIFUL AND MIGHTY
> GOD IN THREE PERSONS
> BLESSED TRINITY!

ABIGAIL *and the audience make up a youth choir.*

YOUTH CHOIR.
   AAAMEN

This final note extends while the guitar begins.

ABIGAIL. I got to meet Mrs Wean a few years before she died. I feel so grateful for every minute I got to spend with her. She was a force on this planet, and we sing this song in her honor.

SHAUN *playing guitar, a bright and introspective sound.*

CARDINALS

SHAUN. NIGHT AT THE CHURCH
   AT REHEARSAL
   MY PALMS SWEAT WHEN I'M SITTING NEXT TO
   THE GIRLS
   IN THE CIRCLE AS WE SPEAK OF JESUS
   LAST SHALL BE FIRST WHEN THE BOYS RACE TO
   BE FIRST IN LINE
   THE GIRLS SHALL BE FIRST, THE BOYS BEHIND

   KAY CONDUCTS THE CHILDREN
   IN THE BLOSSOM OF THE CHORUS
   A SOLO, MY FIRST, A TREE IN A FOREST

THE LIGHTS BEHIND HER HAIR BOUNCE
OFF THE VINYL FLOORING
FLORESCENT LIGHTS, HER FACE ADORING

AND WHAT I WILL REMEMBER
FOREVER
IS A TREE
A TREE LIT UP WITH CARDINALS
SMALL PAINTED WITH THE SNOW
THAT FELL SLOW
IN THE GLOW
OF THE LCD SCREEN
IN THE CHURCH YARD

ALL THE KIDS IN THE YOUTH GROUP
THEY WANNA KNOW WHY I
NEVER SPEAK
NOT A WORD, NOT A WORD TO ANYONE

I CARRY A CROSS
NEXT TO FRIENDS
HOLDING THE CANDLES
MY BODY A TWIG, MY ARMS BROOM HANDLES

THE SMELL OF THE PERFUME
IN THE HALO OF THE MOTHERS

THE WARMTH OF THE MOTHERS
THE COLD OF THE FATHERS

SHE HANDS ME A SCRIPT
WITH MY NAME ON IT
THE FEAR OF WORDS
THE VOID OF SONNETS

AND WHAT I WILL REMEMBER
FOREVER
IS A TREE
A TREE LIT UP WITH CARDINALS
SMALL PAINTED WITH THE SNOW
THAT FELL SLOW
IN THE GLOW
OF THE LCD SCREEN
IN THE CHURCH YARD

I WAS AFRAID TO SING
oh yes

SHAUN.
I WAS AFRAID TO SPEAK

KAY.
I REMEMBER

SHAUN.
BUT I DID IT

KAY.
YOU DID IT!

SHAUN.
MRS WEAN, BECAUSE OF YOU

THE SMELL OF THE BLEACH IN THE AIR
THE BEEPING OF THE ALL LITTLE MACHINES
NEVER SEEM NEVER SEEM TO GO ANYWHERE
HER FACE LOOKS HEAVY, HER HUSBAND LIFTS
   HER UP IN THE BED
WHEN SHE CAN'T SPEAK, HE SPEAKS INSTEAD
ABIGAIL MAKES HER LAUGH WITH
TALK OF MARIJUANA
THE SILENCE BROKEN
GOLDEN SPREADING
I LOOK FOR THE WORDS
THE WORDS THAT NEVER COME
THEY NEVER COME
NEVER COME

I WISH I COULD HAVE THANKED YOU

AND WHAT I WILL REMEMBER
FOREVER
MRS WEAN
A TREE LIT UP WITH CARDINALS
SMALL PAINTED WITH THE SNOW
THAT FELL SLOW
IN THE GLOW
OF THE LCD SCREEN
IN THE CHURCH YARD

SHAUN *takes off his guitar.*

So there I was in Ohio, and singing in church is really how I started making friends – like any friends at all.
So I doubled down. I tripled down. Jesus became my party planner.
I did it all. I did the handbell choir. I was in the puppet ministry. I was Balthazar in *Wise Guys and Starry Skies*… the smash hit of the '96 Christmas Season.
And I was learning that there was a correct way to be a Christian and that I was good at it.
I took it very seriously. I would record my deepest theological ruminations every night in my Garfield the Cat purple hardcover journal.

ABIGAIL *reveals the Garfield journal.*

ABIGAIL. We have here the authentic Garfield journal.

SHAUN. So I'm going to read for you my actual hard-hitting questions. And you will read back the actual answers the congregation gave me. Ready?
Okay, question one:
How did Noah fit the dinosaurs on the Ark, given that they were rather large?
You answer:

CONGREGATION. Dinosaurs aren't real. Their bones were planted by Satan.

SHAUN. Question two: How did Cain and Abel populate the earth if the only woman on the Earth at that time was their mother Eve?
You answer:

CONGREGATION. With Eve.

SHAUN *puts notebook down; he returns to home base.*

SHAUN. And so, doubt crept in.
In the morning I was still singing hymns in church like a good Christian soldier member of Future Pastors of America. But at night I'd be in some garage playing my guitar as loudly as I could with the stoners. I was the only one high on just the music.

And I'd stumble home, drunk on sound. Alone in the night. And that's when I heard something. At first, I thought the cicadas had come early! But it was my ears. The ringing in my ears was getting worse.

So, this is what my tinnitus sounded like when I was fifteen:

A persistent high ringing sound that makes the language a little hard to understand. The captions above the stage start blurring and distorting.

Is that coming through? I can't hear these frequencies anymore. I made this experiment for Abigail to try and explain what it sounds like in my head. Thought this might be useful for you all, too?
It sounds to me like cicadas so I used the sound of cicadas to make this. And the thing with tinnitus, is that any of those tones that you're hearing in your head, those are the frequencies you can no longer hear in the outside world. Consonants are all high-frequency sounds, so I'm losing those first.
So we're going to switch over my mic.

The sound of tinnitus grows.

And now, as the tinnitus progresses, you're going to start losing those frequencies in my microphone and there will be more tinnitus. I mean, I have no idea what you can or can't hear but anyways, here we go…
So the years go by, I'm becoming more and more handsome…

I think this is about what it sounds like in my head right now. Consonants are getting har er to understand.

And as we move into the fu ure, maybe a deca e or so…

[I think this is about what it sounds like in my head right now. Consonants are getting harder to understand.
And as we move into the future, maybe a decade or so…]

Aroun this point was when my da s opped playing music with other peo le
And I think this is abou where my father's ears a e now, and where   y ea s are headi .

So let's roll it back, back to the present, and and...

[Around this point was when my dad stopped playing music with other people
And I think this is about where my father's ears are now, and where my ears are heading.
So let's roll it back, back to the present, and...]

Goodbye, tinnitus.

End of tinnitus experiment.

So, while I was playing in my epic, shitty garage bands, Dad was getting obsessed about protecting my ears. He'd always try to get me to wear ear plugs. He'd leave them all around the house, like bowls of condoms at the Planned Parenthood. And I would wear my ear plugs for like two minutes max because just like condoms they make everything feel worse.

SHAUN *sets up a screen.*

ABIGAIL. We're gonna sing a Shema prayer.
A Shema is a prayer, a Jewish prayer, a prayer of my people. I'm composting a lot of the Judaism I was brought up with right now, but there are some things I love about Judaism and one is that Judaism is a religion of doubt. It loves mystery. The holy texts are filled with rabbis writing in the margins, arguing across centuries, telling jokes across time about the impossibility of a singular meaning for anything. At its heart Judaism is allergic to certainty. Which means it's allergic to fascism. And I just need to say, the most Jewish thing I can imagine doing now is working for the liberation of Palestine.

And I gotta tell you I think Shaun's dad? Doubts like a Jew. So! Shema means 'O Hear.' A Shema prayer is a prayer to hear, to be heard.

And your part is this:

SHEMA

(*Humming.*) SHEMA SHEMA SHEMA

The Shema chant continues.

In Shaun's father's voice, we pray:

ABIGAIL AS JOHN.
> OH HEAR MY SON
> BEFORE YOU GO OUT
> DON'T FORGET YOUR EAR PLUGS
> DON'T TAKE THEM OUT
> OF YOUR PERFECT CURLING EAR
> OH SHAUN
> PROTECT WHAT YOU HOLD DEAR
>
> SHEMA SHEMA SHEMA
>
> OH HEAR, MY SON
> MY OLDEST ONE
> MY SAPLING TREE
> YOU ARE OF ME
>
> SHEMA SHEMA SHEMA

The Shema chant continues.

SHAUN *sets up a projector and pulls out transparencies.*

So the thing that allows you to hear is the smallest organ in your body. Here she is –

Projector turns on.

– it's your cochlea! It's the size of a garden pea. It's filled with liquid, and it's shaped like a snail shell. It spirals back and back. It's your cochlea!

Your cochlea is lined with tiny ear cells. They stand in perfect formation, like a choir, ready to sing. Or sometimes, they take the shape of a pipe organ. These are your stereocilia! And they are responsible for every single frequency you hear.

Each stereocilia is responsible for absorbing a frequency from the outside world through your ear canal and ringing the bell of that frequency in your brain. If you don't have a stereocilia that matches that frequency, then you can't hear that frequency.

And if your stereocilia become damaged, they will bow down to the earth.

And when they've done that, they've died.
This could happen from a blast, from a fever, from genetics, from a war.
Once your stereocilia have died they will never come back.

But! Although they can no longer ring the bell of that frequency in your brain, from the outside world, they will tell your brain that the frequency they are responsible for is ringing – forever.
And we *think* that this is tinnitus.
It's the afterlife of an ear cell.
It's the singing of the choir of stereocilia. After they've died.

SHAUN *returns to home base and puts on his guitar.*

ABIGAIL & SHAUN AS JOHN.
> INSIDE YOUR INNER EAR
> CURLED LIKE A SNAIL
> THERE IS A CONGREGATION
> OF TINY SAPLINGS
> THE INNER ANATOMY
> OF YOUR EAR
> IS INVISIBLE
> AND IMPOSSIBLE TO HEAR
> UNTIL IT GETS INJURED MY DEAR
>
> SHEMA SHEMA OH HEAR
>
> THEY STAND IN ROWS
> SINGING WHEN THEY'RE TOLD
> THEY STAND IN ROWS
> SINGING WHEN THEY'RE TOLD

This is repeated and grows and grows.

> SHEMA SHEMA DAYANU

ABIGAIL AS JOHN.
> BUT WHEN A BLAST COMES
> OH SOME WILL SUCCUMB
> TAKE CARE TAKE CARE
> OF THE WEAKEST ONES
>
> WHEN A BLAST COMES
> OH SOME WILL SUCCUMB

>   TAKE CARE TAKE CARE
>   OF THE WEAKEST ONES
>
>   SHEMA SHEMA DAYANU

SHAUN. This was my dad's last sermon. He did not know it was going to be his last sermon at the time that he gave it. But it turned out to be a real conversation starter in Dayton, Ohio, in the nineties.

O COURAGE

ABIGAIL.
>   OH COURAGE
>   OH COURAGE
>   OH BRING ME COURAGE
>
>   SOME OF YOU KNOW
>   I'VE HAD TO STEP BACK FROM THE COMMUNITY SHOW
>   AND THOUGH BRIAN WILL BE A BRILLIANT TEVYA
>   I WAS SORRY TO SEE IT GO
>   SOME OF YOU KNOW
>   I AM LOSING MY HEARING
>   MANY THINGS ARE DISAPPEARING
>   FOR ME NOW
>   BUT SOMETHING ELSE
>   IS COMING CLOSER SOMEHOW
>
>   NOW I'D BE LYING IF I SAID
>   THAT I WAS NOT AFRAID
>   AND I'D BE LYING IF I SAID
>   THAT I KNEW HOW TO PRAY
>   BUT MY FRIENDS I HAVE SOMETHING
>   THAT I HAVE TO SAY
>   ANYWAY
>
>   THERE IS NO HELL
>   THERE IS NO HELL
>   AND NO MATTER WHAT YOU DO MY FRIENDS
>   THERE WILL BE NO HELL FOR YOU
>
>   OH FRIENDS
>   WE PUNISH ONE ANOTHER

AND SAY GOD HAS TOLD US TO
WE PUNISH ONE ANOTHER
OH YES AND I HAVE DONE IT TOO

BUT OH MY FRIENDS
MY FRIENDS
I'D LIKE TO TRY SOMETHING NEW

OH COURAGE

AND IF THERE IS A HEAVEN
THE POSSIBILITY OF HEAVEN
IT'S ONLY NOW
IT'S IN THIS WORLD
NOT ANOTHER
IT'S BETWEEN YOU AND YOUR BROTHER
AND THE MOMENTS WHEN THE SPACE BETWEEN
  DISSOLVES

AND IF WE WANT A HEAVEN
WE BETTER MAKE IT NOW

SO COURAGE
TAKE COURAGE
BRING ME
COURAGE

SHAUN. His congregation *hated* this!
His congregation *hated* this so much.
They hated it so much they made a committee about hating it, which you may not know is the most damning form of action you can take in the Midwest!
They committee'd him right out of that church, right out of Capital C Church altogether.
And I looked around at all these people that I had tried so hard to please, that I had wanted to be, and my stomach changed.

Meanwhile I was going to these concerts that were *destroying* my ears.
But they were also cracking me open
And something new was pouring forth.

Okay, over the course of this next song, I'm going to become an atheist.

A swirling cascading beat.

THESE ROADS

    I WOULDN'T EVER
    I'D NEVER THINK
    I WOULDN'T EVER
    I'D NEVER THINK
    I WOULDN'T EVER
    I'D NEVER THINK

    ALL MY LIFE
    I'VE DRIVEN THESE ROADS IN
    THE SUMMER
    I'VE KILLED MANY THINGS WITH MY BODY
    I'M LEAVING BEHIND ME
    THE SOULS OF A THOUSAND AND
    ONE SMALL THINGS

    I TAKE IN A BREATH AND
    I BREATHE OUT THE CARBON
    THAT BROKE UP WITHIN ME
    I'M LEAVING BEHIND ME
    THE SOULS OF A THOUSAND AND ONE SMALL
        THINGS

SHAUN & ABIGAIL.
    ALL MY LIFE
    I'VE DRIVEN THESE ROADS IN
    THE SUMMER I HEARD YOU THERE
    BREATHING BESIDE ME I
    HEARD SOMEONE SPEAKING
    ABOUT ALL THE GIFTS OF THE GARDEN

    I DRAPED THEM UPON ME
    THE BODIES
    THE BODIES OF MANY A SPIRIT
    I'M LEAVING BEHIND ME
    THE SOULS OF A THOUSAND AND ONE SMALL
        THINGS

SHAUN.
    I WOULDN'T EVER
    I'D NEVER THINK

I WOULDN'T EVER
I'D NEVER THINK
I WOULDN'T EVER
I'D NEVER THINK

SHAUN & ABIGAIL.
ALL MY LIFE OH
EVEN IN MY YOUTH
OH EVEN IN MY YOUTH
I WAS EATING OF THE FRUIT
I WAS EATING THE FRUIT UP
I ATE IT ALL UP
I THREW AWAY THE SEEDS

EVEN IN MY YOUTH
OH EVEN IN MY YOUTH
I WAS EATING OF THE FRUIT
I WAS EATING THE FRUIT UP
I ATE IT ALL UP
I THREW AWAY THE SEEDS

ALL MY LIFE
I'VE DRIVEN THESE ROADS IN
THE SUMMER
I'VE KILLED MANY THINGS WITH MY BODY
I'M LEAVING BEHIND ME
THE SOULS OF A THOUSAND AND
ONE SMALL THINGS

THE BONES OF THE OLD ONES TURN INTO
THE OIL THAT SHAKES UP THE GROUND
IS THERE
WAITING TO BURN UP
TO BURN UP THE WHOLE WORLD AROUND

I AM LIVING THE LIFE OF THE ASH OF THE FIRE
THAT STARTED IN CLEVELAND
THE HUSK OF THE RIND OF
THE FACTORY LINE OF OUR HENRY FORD

OH
EVEN IN MY YOUTH OH
EVEN IN MY YOUTH
I WAS EATING OF THE FRUIT

> I WAS EATING THE FRUIT UP
> OH I ATE IT ALL UP
> I THREW AWAY THE SEEDS
>
> EVEN IN MY YOUTH OH
> EVEN IN MY YOUTH
> I WAS EATING OF THE FRUIT
> I WAS EATING THE FRUIT UP
> OH I ATE IT ALL UP
> I THREW IT AWAY

Soundscape – a wild chant grows.

> YEA YEA YAAI AAI
> YEA YEA YAAI AAI
> YEA YEA YAAI AAI

ABIGAIL. I'm about to meet Shaun
So we're just gonna pause here and in the length of one song I'm gonna catch you up on everything about my life up to this point.

WORMS

> WHEN I WAS A GIRL I WAS ANNOYING
> NOT LIKE NOW
> I'D SING ALL THE TIME
> AND MY MOTHER DIDN'T MIND
> BUT SHE DID SEND ME OUTSIDE
> FOR LONG STRETCHES AT A TIME
> WHICH IS WHERE I FOUND MY FIRST PET
> WHICH WAS AN EARTHWORM
> I HELD HER IN MY HAND AND SANG TO HER AND
>   I FELT SHE COULD UNDERSTAND ME
> THEN I'D SLIP HER BACK INTO THE EARTH
> TAKING ALL MY SONGS WITH HER
> AND THE NEXT DAY I'D DO THE SAME
> ANOTHER WORM MAYBE
> THOUGH CALLED BY THE SAME NAME
> AND WHEN THERE WAS NO WORM
> I'D SING TO DIRT AND IT COMFORTED ME
> AND THIS IS HOW I LEARNED TO SING TO WHAT
>   I COULD NOT SEE

LESS LIKE A PET
MORE LIKE A GOD
INVISIBLE BUT LISTENING LOVING ME AND
   ALWAYS THERE TINY GOD OF EARTH AND
   SHIT GOD THAT COULD TAKE MY PAIN AND
   COMPOST IT

WHEN MY BROTHER DIED
MY MOTHER ASKED US
WHERE DID HE GO
WHERE DID HE GO
MY LITTLE ONE MY ONLY SON
WHERE DID HE GO
AND ONCE AGAIN I HAD TO ANSWER OH I'M
   SORRY
I DON'T KNOW
BUT I'M PRETTY SURE HES FOOD FOR WORMS

OH WORM!
EATER OF THE DEAD!
COMPOSTER OF THE DETRITUS OF THE WORLD
SHE WHO DANCES IN HOPPING CIRCLES WHEN
   SHE'S SCARED
SHE WHO LETS HER LONG BODY STRETCH EVEN
   THOUGH SHE'S DELICIOUS TO MOST LIVING
   THINGS
WHO HAS NO EYES TO SEE
WHOSE BODY IS A LONG TONGUE COVERED IN
   TASTEBUDS
WHO COULD NOT HEAR MY SONG BUT TASTED IT
WHO SURFACES TO WITNESS RAIN EVEN
   THOUGH IT KILLS HER
WHAT CREATURE TELL ME LOVES LIFE MORE?
OH MY MOTHER
MY BROTHER HE'S FOOD FOR WORMS
FOOD FOR GOD
SO GOD CAN GROW
FOOD FOR GOD
SO GOD CAN GROW

(*Spoken.*) And then I met Shaun. And when I met Shaun he was an *atheist.*

    Like even the mention of organized religion, or church or prayer of any kind made him actively enraged.

SHAUN. It's true! It would get me *pissed*!

ABIGAIL. He was only interested in religious figures insofar as they were also revolutionary figures. In fact this was his pick-up line for me:

SHAUN. Get out your notebooks, gentlemen.

ABIGAIL. His pick-up line was 'Jesus was an activist.' And it totally worked.
Coming from where I come from, like a Jewish Pagan Witch, all the Jesus talk was very foreign and erotic to me.
So then I was pregnant.
And I called my grandmother, and I asked, 'What's it going to be like to give birth?'
She had been pregnant fifteen times – she had ten living children.
She said, 'Honey, it's not a big deal. It was like having a really, really big poop.'
No, it's not. It's not like that at all. She lied to me. It's so much worse than that.

So I was in labor. I was in labor a really long time.

SHAUN. And I was up behind her on the bed, and for some reason I had decided to wear skinny jeans to the hospital. So I just got this wild chafe from one knee through my crotch and down to the other knee.
Just…
I was suffering, too – that's all I'm trying to say!

ABIGAIL. It turns out that the cord was wrapped around the baby's neck, and he was turned in such a way that I would push him out, and then the cord would pull him back in.

Somewhere around hour twenty-six of labor I had an experience. I had a vision.
I saw Shaun's ancestry come into the room.

SHAUN. No thank you. We'd like a clean-slate baby, please.

ABIGAIL. His grandfathers, and great-grandfather, and back and back and back.

SHAUN. Nope! Please take your weird traditions and genetics and go.

ABIGAIL. They were knocking on the door of my body
And asking to be born

LINE OF FATHERS

THERE IS A LINE OF FATHERS
JUST BEHIND MY SHOULDERS
I CAN FEEL THEIR BREATH ON MY NECK
THEY'RE MARCHING TOWARDS THE BORDERS
FROM THAT WORLD TO THE NEXT
GETTING YOUNGER
GETTING YOUNGER WITH EVERY STEP
CAN I COME IN, THEY ASK

The voices of the ancestors sing.

SHAUN (*as ancestors*).
I REMEMBER THE TASTE OF APPLES
I REMEMBER THE SOUND OF RAIN

ABIGAIL.
CAN I COME IN? THEY ASK

SHAUN.
I REMEMBER THE LAP OF MY MOTHER
I'VE FORGOTTEN MY MOTHER'S NAME

ABIGAIL.
BY THE TIME I CAN SEE THEM
THEY HAVE BECOME CHILDREN
WHO'VE FORGOTTEN
ALL BUT THE WATER IN THEIR MOUTHS

YES I WILL WALTZ WITH THE LIVING
YES I WILL WALTZ WITH THE DEAD
WHEN I LIFT HIM UP
WHEN I SMELL MY BABY'S HEAD

OH CAN I COME IN, THEY ASK

SHAUN.
>I REMEMBER THE SOUND OF THUNDER
>I REMEMBER THE FEEL OF THE RAIN

ABIGAIL.
>CAN I COME IN? THEY ASK

SHAUN.
>I REMEMBER THE LAP OF MY MOTHER
>I'VE FORGOTTEN MY MOTHER'S NAME

ABIGAIL.
>THE LINE IS SO LONG IT'S A CIRCLE
>AND THE CIRCLE'S SO DEEP IT'S A WAVE
>AND THE WAVES MOVE INTO YOUR BODY
>GIRL THAT'S HOW A BABY IS MADE
>OH THE LINE IS SO LONG IT'S A CIRCLE
>AND THE CIRCLE'S SO DEEP IT'S A WAVE
>AND THE WAVES MOVE INTO YOUR BODY
>GIRL THAT'S HOW A BABY IS MADE
>OH THE LINE IS SO LONG IT'S A CIRCLE
>AND THE CIRCLE'S SO DEEP IT'S A WAVE
>AND THE WAVES MOVE INTO YOUR BODY
>GIRL THAT'S HOW A BABY IS MADE

ABIGAIL & SHAUN.
>CAN I COME IN? WE ASK

ABIGAIL.
>THIS IS WHAT I CARRY
>NOT A BABY
>BUT A WORLD

SHAUN.
>CAN I COME IN? WE ASK

ABIGAIL.
>THIS IS WHAT I CARRY
>IN THIS BODY OF A GIRL
>CAN I COME IN? THEY ASK

ABIGAIL & SHAUN.
>OH THIS IS WHAT WE CARRY
>YES THE FUTURE
>YES THE PAST

ABIGAIL.
>WALTZING BRIEFLY IN A MOMENT
>IN A FEVER
>THAT CAN'T LAST

SHAUN. Something's wrong. Something is wrong.
>The baby is born, but he can't breathe.
>They put him in this six-foot-long plastic tube and rush him off in an ambulance to a bigger hospital thirty miles away.
>They put Abigail in her own ambulance and she's gone. They won't let me in with either of them! So I follow behind.
>And when we get to the new hospital, we are thrust into this new plane of existence,
>this in-between world.

SHAUN goes to the mobile projector.

Reality shifts.

A rumbling underwater sound.

ABIGAIL. The NICU. the Neonatal Intensive Care Unit. Not the land of the living, not the land of the dead.
>There used to be an ocean in Ohio.
>Everyone is born underwater. For the first year of your life you're aquatic! In your mother's womb. Then you're born. The first thing you have to learn how to do is breathe, which our son can't do.

I came into the room and saw my baby stretched out on the table –
>He needed an IV, so they were trying to put a needle in his arm,
>But it's a teaching hospital, so they were *training* someone how to do this.
>They can't get it so they're sticking him again and again and again
>My baby is using what little breath he has to scream and cry
>Finally I say 'GET THE FUCK AWAY FROM MY BABY'
>And I turn to Shaun and say:

(******inaudible******)

SHAUN *turns off the sinkhole.*

SHAUN. She's trying to tell me something, but I can't
understand it
Everyone is trying to tell me important things about my baby
and I can't understand any of them.
I haven't slept for days at this point
My tinnitus gets out of control when I don't sleep
I can't tune it out
And all of tools – my lip reading, my context clues – none of
it is working
I retreat further and further into myself
Until I feel locked in like I did when I was a boy.
Alone. Ashamed.
I've given my boy this body, *my* body – and it's failing him.
And I don't know what to do.

I used to have a playbook, a way to handle times like this
I used to know that in this moment I could pray, but I don't
have prayers anymore

SHAUN *picks up his guitar.*

I listen for that old voice, the voice of my God – but all
I hear is a ringing that I can't tune out
And all I've got is this ache around a void

I KEPT MY HEART

OH, I LISTENED TO THE AIR
I WAS ONCE FOUND THERE
THE GHOST OF A THOUGHT
OF A THOUGHT, OF A THOUGHT
OF A SOMEONE, OF A SOMETHING
LAID UPON A BLANKET OF A THOUSAND
 THREADS
OF THE THREADS OF A MOMENT OF THE SKIN OF
 AN EYE
OF SILENCE WARM AND STILL
OH
I DON'T KNOW WHAT WAS THERE, BUT I KNOW
 IT'S GONE AWAY

THE CLUTCH OF RIBBONS IN MY CHEST
THE WISH TO KNOW SOME REST
THE TIREDNESS THREADS, IT THREADS

IT THREADS, IT THREADS
IT THREADS MY BONES
I HAD A BIRD OF A WISH
OF A WISH I'D SHOUTED THAT I HAD CALLED MY OWN
AND OF ALL THE SILENCE THAT ANSWERED ME OH
I DON'T KNOW WHAT WAS THERE, BUT I KNOW IT'S GONE AWAY

THE METER OF A THOUGHT
THE WEIGHT OF ALL I'M NOT
THE THINGS I'VE TIED, I'VE TIED
AROUND MY CHEST, MY CHEST, MY NECK
THE TREASURES OF A SHIP, OF A SHIP THAT WRECKED
AND SPREAD ITS SHININGS ROUND
I WATCHED AS IT TUMBLED DOWN
OH, I'D BE LYING IF I SAID THAT I WAS NOT AFRAID
I'D BE LYING IF I SAID THAT I KNEW HOW TO PRAY
BUT THE PRAYERS GO OUT AND ARE
SWALLOWED BY THE DAY
SO I TURNED AWAY, I TURNED AWAY
SO I TURNED AWAY, I TURNED AWAY
SO I TURNED AWAY, I TURNED AWAY

SHAUN *takes his guitar off.*

About a year after our son was born, I was holding Louie on the couch in our little apartment in Queens. I had YouTube on for him even though watching TV turns one hundred percent of children into cocaine addicts.

It was this really difficult time in our life, both our families were falling apart, people weren't talking to each other, and we were performing a lot, so my ears were degrading very rapidly.
I was just so overwhelmed in every aspect of my life.

I noticed that Louie was mostly into it for the flashing lights. So I turned down the volume, and I just sat there. With him. And in that silence, my tinnitus expanded and expanded

But I didn't try to tune it out, I just let it get big
And then there was this tingling sensation
This wash of love that swept over my whole body
And I heard this small voice out from the middle of the ringing in my ears that said:

We have never forgotten you, Shaun.
We have always been here
Loving you.

And that was it. That's what I got.
For the next year, I'd discover my face was wet, find out I had been crying?
Like, in public places – on the subway, in a café, at rehearsal.
And it all made me wonder
Who the hell was this we?
God? The holy trinity? Lots of gods? Neighbors with open arms and jello salads? The creatures of the creek? The choir of the stereocilia themselves?

What's happening to me?
My dad used to sing to me, when I was afraid of the ringing
Then we sang together.
He doesn't sing anymore

How long will I be able to do any of this?

ABIGAIL *builds the loop with the audience, everyone becoming the stereocilia.*

REQUIEM

ABIGAIL *sings the wordless Requiem chant.*

Then repeats and continues under the following as the music continues:

SHAUN. What's going to happen to me?
I asked my father.

Dad?

ABIGAIL. Yes.

SHAUN. Can you hear –
Can you hear the shake of coins in the pocket?

The faucet drip?
The neighbor's voice through the wall?

ABIGAIL. No.

SHAUN. The dog far away?

ABIGAIL. No.

SHAUN. The flirt
The wink
The subtle joke?

ABIGAIL. No. No.

SHAUN. Bird calls?

ABIGAIL. No.

SHAUN. The voice of your daughter?

ABIGAIL. No.

SHAUN. The soft moan?
The gentle chuckle?
The thrush, the linnet, the bumblebee?
The gentle part of an overture?
Jokes?

ABIGAIL. No.

SHAUN. Punchlines?
So many quiet asides from friends?
The moment someone says something at the restaurant to only you in a low, conspiratorial tone and then pulls back to see your reaction on your face?

ABIGAIL. No.

SHAUN. Timing?

ABIGAIL. No.

SHAUN. Everything above C
Above high C?

ABIGAIL. No.
No, can you?

SHAUN. A little, still.
Can you hear the place where the band is in the score?
The moment of all starting together
Singing with abandon and in control at the same time?

ABIGAIL. No. No. No.

SHAUN. My mother's voice?

ABIGAIL. Mom's voice?
No, not really.

SHAUN. The elderly shake of voice?

ABIGAIL. No.

SHAUN. The brush of cotton on clean skin?

ABIGAIL. No.

SHAUN. The low rumble of thunder?

ABIGAIL. No.

SHAUN. Can you hear the hiss of gas left on?
The tick of the turn signal?

ABIGAIL. No.

SHAUN. The voice of God?

ABIGAIL. Yes.

SHAUN. The myriad voices of God?

ABIGAIL. No.

SHAUN. The mad diversity of gods?

ABIGAIL. No.

SHAUN. The cacophony of God, the pattern in the chaos,
which is no pattern but more chaos?

ABIGAIL. No.

SHAUN. The possibility of meaning?

ABIGAIL. Yes.

SHAUN. Can you hear the quiet voice of your grandson?

ABIGAIL. No.

SHAUN. The voice of your mother since her passing?

ABIGAIL. No.
No, ask me again.

SHAUN. The voice of your mother since her passing?

ABIGAIL. Yes.

SHAUN. The quiet voice of God?

ABIGAIL. Yes.

SHAUN. The voice of your son, at the pulpit, on the stage?

ABIGAIL. Yes.
Do you remember me at the pulpit?

SHAUN. Yes.

ABIGAIL. Can you still hear that?

SHAUN. Yes.
The choir singing loud?

ABIGAIL. Yes.
The clap?

SHAUN. Yes.

ABIGAIL. The joyful noise?

SHAUN. Yes.

ABIGAIL. The great pool of stillness below your chest?

SHAUN. Yes.

ABIGAIL. The drop of a stone in that pool?

SHAUN. Yes.

ABIGAIL. The chord struck and still ringing?

SHAUN. Yes.
The call of my great-great-great-grandfathers across the ocean?

ABIGAIL. Yes.

SHAUN. The cruelty of our history?

ABIGAIL. Yes.
  The blessing?

SHAUN. Yes.
  Yes.

ABIGAIL. Dad?

SHAUN. Yeah, Louie?

ABIGAIL. Can you hear me?

SHAUN. Pardon?

ABIGAIL. Can you hear me?

SHAUN. Yes.

ABIGAIL. Can I have some milk?

SHAUN. Yes.

ABIGAIL. Can I have some Legos?

SHAUN. Yes.

ABIGAIL. Can I sleep in your bed?
  [Can I sleep in your bed?]

SHAUN. Yes.
  [Yes.]

ABIGAIL. Can I go to my friend's?
  [Can I go to my friend's?]

SHAUN. Yes.
  [Yes.]

ABIGAIL. Can I borrow the car?
  [Can I borrow the car?]

SHAUN. Yes.
  [Yes.]

ABIGAIL. Can I borrow the car?
  [Can I borrow the car?]

OHIO 39

SHAUN. No.

[No.]

ABIGAIL. Can you help me move?

[Can you help me move?]

SHAUN. Yes.

[Yes.]

ABIGAIL. Can you come to graduation?

[Can you come to graduation?]

SHAUN. Yes.

[Yes.]

ABIGAIL. Could you hear my speech?

[Could you hear my speech?]

SHAUN. Most of it.

[Most of it.]

ABIGAIL. Do you need a hand?

[Do you need a hand?]

SHAUN. No.

[No.]

ABIGAIL. Do you need a hand?

[Do you need a hand?]

SHAUN. Yes.

[Yes.]

ABIGAIL. Are you comfortable here?

[Are you comfortable here?]

SHAUN. Yes.

[Yes.]

ABIGAIL. Can I get you some water?

[Can I get you some water?]

SHAUN. Yes.

[Yes.]

ABIGAIL. Do you need more pain meds?

[Do you need more pain meds?]

SHAUN. No.

[No.]

ABIGAIL. Are you comfortable, Dad?

[Are you comfortable, Dad?]

SHAUN. Yes.

[Yes.]

ABIGAIL. Dad?

Dad?

Dad?

[Dad?
Dad?
Dad?]

SHAUN *goes to the projector.*

Can you hear me?

Can you hear me?

Can you hear me?

[Can you hear me?
Can you hear me?
Can you hear me?]

SHAUN *slowly spins the projector so that the light illuminates the faces of the audience.*

Blackout.

That was the end.
But we're going to play one more song.
You didn't think there was nothing after the end?

SHAKE ME

SHAUN.
> CAN YOU HEAR THEM CALLING?
> (*Echo.*)
>
> OUT IN THE QUIET
> COLD IN THE RAIN
> I'D LIKE TO TRY IT
> TO HEAR MY NEW NAME
>
> JOSHUA CALLED FOR AN ANSWER
> AN ANSWER NEVER CAME
> I CAN HEAR HIM CALLING
> HIS TRUMPET PLAYS MY NAME
>
> SOMETIMES IT DON'T BLOW HARD ENOUGH
> AND I AM LEFT COATED IN DUST
> SO SHAKE ME HARD, PULL ME NEAR
> THROUGH THE RINGING IN MY BROKEN EARS
> THERE IS SINGING

ABIGAIL & SHAUN.
> IF ONLY I COULD HEAR IT
>
> CAN YOU HEAR THEM WAILING?
> (*Echo.*)
> LOSE MY BEAUTY LOSE MY STRENGTH
> AND I'VE JUST BEGUN!
> I'LL GIVE AWAY THIS BODY
> BY THE TIME I'M DONE!
>
> SALT FROM THE WATER
> APPLE FROM THE TREE
> I'LL BE SO MUCH SMALLER
> WILL YOU
> WILL YOU COME CLOSE TO ME?
>
> SOMETIMES IT DON'T BLOW HARD ENOUGH
> AND I AM LEFT COATED IN DUST
> SO SHAKE ME HARD, PULL ME NEAR
> THROUGH THE RINGING IN THESE BROKEN EARS
> THERE IS SINGING
> THERE IS SINGING

> IF ONLY I COULD HEAR IT
> OH THE JOYFUL NOISE
> OH THE JOYFUL NOISE

ABIGAIL.
> OH THE JOYFUL, JOYFUL NOISE

ALL.
> OH THE JOYFUL, JOYFUL NOISE

Loop, repeat.

End of show.

A Nick Hern Book

Ohio first published in Great Britain in 2025 as a paperback original by Nick Hern Books Limited, The Glasshouse, 49a Goldhawk Road, London W12 8QP, in association with Francesca Moody Productions, piece by piece productions and the Young Vic

Ohio copyright © 2025 Shaun McClain Bengson and Abigail Nessen Bengson

The Bengsons have asserted their moral right to be identified as the authors of this work

Cover design: feastcreative.com; photography: Oliver Rosser

Designed and typeset by Nick Hern Books, London
Printed in the UK by Mimeo Ltd, Huntingdon, Cambridgeshire PE29 6XX

A CIP catalogue record for this book is available from the British Library

ISBN 978 1 83904 534 9

CAUTION Professionals and amateurs are hereby warned that *Ohio* is subject to a royalty. It is fully protected under the copyright laws of the United States of America and of all countries covered by the International Copyright Union (including the Dominion of Canada and the rest of the British Commonwealth), the Berne Convention, the Pan-American Copyright Convention and the Universal Copyright Convention as well as all countries with which the United States has reciprocal copyright relations. All rights, including professional/ amateur stage rights, motion picture, recitation, lecturing, public reading, radio broadcasting, television, video or sound recording, all other forms of mechanical or electronic reproduction, such as CD-ROM, CD-I, information storage and retrieval systems and photocopying, and the rights of translation into foreign languages, are strictly reserved. Particular emphasis is laid upon the matter of readings, permission for which must be secured from the Author's agent in writing. Inquiries concerning rights should be addressed to: William Morris Endeavor Entertainment, LLC, 11 Madison Avenue, 18th Floor, New York, New York 10010, USA; attn: Michael Finkle

www.nickhernbooks.co.uk/environmental-policy

Nick Hern Books' authorised representative in the EU is
Easy Access System Europe – Mustamäe tee 50, 10621 Tallinn, Estonia
email gpsr.requests@easproject.com

www.nickhernbooks.co.uk

@nickhernbooks